Football Crazy

Sheila M. Blackburn

The first book in Set A of
Sam's Football Stories

Dedication
For my Mum.
With thanks to Tom for all the support and understanding.

Acknowledgements
With thanks to *The Boots Company* and *Delmar Press in Nantwich*, for their support of this project.

Published by Brilliant Publications
Unit 10, Sparrow Hall Farm
Edlesborough
Dunstable
Bedfordshire
LU6 2ES, UK

General information enquiries:
Tel: 01525 222292
Website: www.brilliantpublications.co.uk

The name Brilliant Publications and the logo are registered trademarks.

Written by Sheila M. Blackburn
Illustrated by Tony O'Donnell of Graham Cameron Illustration
© Sheila M. Blackburn 2002

Printed ISBN: 9781903853016
e-pdf ISBN: 9780857476142

ISBN 9781903853191 Set A - 6 titles: Football Crazy, Team Talk, Will Monday Ever Come?, Training Night, If Only Dad Could See Us! and a Place on the Team.
ISBN 9781903853030 Set B - 6 titles: The First Match, Trouble for Foz, What about the Girls?, What's Worrying Eddie?, Nowhere to Train and Are We the Champions?

First Published 2002. Reprinted 2006, 2009, 2015.
10 9 8 7 6 5 4

The right of Sheila Blackburn to be identified as the author of this work has been asserted by herself in accordance with the Copyright, Designs and Patents Act 1988.

All rights reserved. No part of this publication may be reproduced, stored in a retrieval system, or transmitted in any form, or by any means electronic, mechanical, photocopying, recording or otherwise, without prior permission from the publisher.

Sam's Football Stories

Sam was football crazy.
Everybody said so.

Gran asked him what he wanted for his birthday.

"A football, please," said Sam.
"I want to be in a football team."

"I think I'll just get the football," said Gran.

Football Crazy

His aunt asked,
"What do you want your cake to look like, Sam?"

"Like a football pitch …
I wish I could play on a real pitch,
and I wish I could play in a real team."

"What sort of party shall we have?" Dad asked.

"A football party, please," said Sam.
"I knew it!" said Dad.

"He's football crazy," they all said.

Dad planned a football quiz,
a goal shooting game,
spot the ball,
and a football treasure trail.

Dad had a good time, but he couldn't think how
to get a team for Sam.

Mum made gingerbread biscuits and iced them in United's colours.

Sam was very happy – except for the team.

"Great, Mum. Thanks," he said.

"You're football crazy," said Mum.
"Can't you think of anything else?"

"No," said Sam, and he ate a little football cake.

It was always the same with Sam.

At school, his teacher told him to write about Three Magic Wishes.

That was easy!

Sam put:

My three magic wishes:
I wish to meet the United team.
I wish to play for England when I grow up.
I wish to be in a football team now.

"I really wanted a longer story, Sam," said Miss Hill.

Sam felt a bit sorry.
He liked Miss Hill.
She did football with the juniors.

He looked at his feet.
"Sorry, Miss," he said, "but those are my three wishes."

"I see," said Miss Hill.
"The trouble with you Sam, is – you're football crazy!"

At Christmas, Sam wrote to Santa.

"What did you put in your letter?" asked Mum.

Sam showed her.

She read:

Dear Santa
I'd like a United kit and I'd like to be in a football team now, because I can't wait until I'm older.

Love from
Sam

"I think the kit will be OK for Santa," said Mum, "but I don't think he can cope with a whole team, Sam."

Football Crazy

On Christmas morning, Sam was very excited.

He got a United kit and put it on at once.
It fitted very well.

He wore it when he opened his other presents:

football books,

football games,

a football pencil case,

a football watch,

a football video,

and a football bed cover.

He didn't take the kit off all day.

He was still wearing it when Gran
and his aunt and uncle came for dinner.

"Did you like the books?" they asked.

"Yes – thank you," said Sam.

"We thought so, because we know
you're football crazy!" said Sam's uncle.

Everybody laughed.

In the New Year, Mum and Dad
went to school to look at Sam's work.

Sam went with them after tea.

He showed them his books,
his football pictures on the wall
and the football models he had made in clay.

When they went to talk to Miss Hill,
Sam had to go to wait in the Library.

Some other children were waiting in there too.
The Head was keeping an eye on them all.

"Choose a book to read," he said.

Sam went to the shelf on Sport.
He found a football book.

Mr Bond shook his head.
"I knew you would, Sam," he said.
"You're football crazy!"

On the way home, Mum and Dad told Sam that Miss Hill had said some good things about his school work.

"You must try to think more about your lessons and less about football," said Dad.

"I do try," said Sam.

"Good," said Dad. "Shall we get some pop and crisps from Mrs Ford's shop?"

They walked on a bit further.

"Sam," said Mum quietly.

"Yes, Mum?"

"You must stop bothering people about this football team idea."

"We didn't know you had asked Miss Hill," said Dad.

"I ask everybody I know," said Sam.

"Miss Hill can't help you Sam," said Mum.
"She has a lot of other things to do."

"I know. She told me," said Sam.

They got to Mrs Ford's corner shop and went in.
Sam picked the pop and crisps.
They waited for Mrs Ford to serve them.

"Miss Hill takes us for football,"
Sam told his Mum and Dad.
"Mr Bond is too old.
There's no one else to do it."

"She still can't run a team for you," said Dad.

He looked at Sam.

"I'm sorry I can't help, Sam.
You know I have to work a lot."

"I know," said Sam.

Sam's Football Stories

Sam put the pop and crisps by
Mrs Ford's till.

"Hello, Sam," said Mrs Ford.
"What's this I hear about a team?"

Mrs Ford liked to chat.
She knew all the news.

"I just want to play in a real football team,"
Sam told her.
"If only there was one around here for boys
my age."

Mrs Ford nodded.

"Don't worry about him, Mrs Ford," said Dad.
"He's football crazy. That's all."

The next day was Friday.
At the end of school, Sam walked home with his best friend, Danny.

There was an old can in the gutter.

Sam kicked it along.

"You doing much this weekend, Sam?"

"Dunno."

"Same here. Meet you down at the wasteland, then, for a game of footie?"

"Yeah. Maybe. See you."

Danny went in through his door.

Sam went on, kicking the can as he ran.

Football Crazy

He got to his house.
There was an old bike against the wall.

He went inside.
Mum was talking to a young man in the kitchen.
"Hello, Sam. This is Eddie – Mrs Ford's son."

"Hi," said Sam.

"Hello, Sam."

Eddie was tall and had a nice smile.

"Eddie has something to ask you."

"My mum tells me you're football crazy," said Eddie.

"Everyone says so," said Sam.
He went very red.

"Me too," said Eddie. "Always have been. So I know what it's like."

"Really?" said Sam.

He looked at his mum. She was smiling.

"The thing is," Eddie went on,
"I'm doing PE at college, and I would like to do
a bit extra in my spare time."

"Extra?" Sam was puzzled.

"Extra PE – football mostly.
Then my mum told me that you had come
into the shop last night.
She said you were talking about a team."

Sam looked hard at Eddie.

"A team?" he said.
"Yes, Sam," said Mum.
"Eddie has come to say he will start a football team
with you and your friends."

Sam gasped. "Really?"

Football Crazy

"Yes, really, Sam," said Mum.
"What do you think?"

"Great! That's just ... great!"

It was all Sam could say.
He was so surprised.

Eddie laughed, but he went on to say:
"I'm going to ask about a place to train each week
and I'll find out about joining a league –
but we need a few others, Sam.
You must talk to your friends."

Football Crazy

"Wow!" said Sam.
He put his coat on again.

"Where are you going?" asked Mum.

"To tell Danny," said Sam.
"There's Rob and Mouse and the others, too."

"Tell them your mum says we can meet here at 7 o'clock on Monday," said Eddie.

"Tell them to bring their parents, if they can make it."

"I will, Eddie – thanks – I'll tell them all."

Sam ran out of the house. The door banged behind him.

Mum laughed. "There you are, Eddie. What did I tell you? He's crazy!"

"Yes," said Eddie. "He's football crazy!"

Football Crazy

We hope that you enjoyed this book. To find out what happens next, look for the next book in the series.

Set A
- Football Crazy
- Team Talk
- Will Monday Ever Come?
- Training Night
- If Only Dad Could See Us!
- A Place on the Team

Set B
- The First Match
- Trouble for Foz
- What about the Girls?
- What's Worrying Eddie?
- Nowhere to Train
- Are We the Champions?